Jesus the Child

Edited by Ken Ham

Original text: Albert Hari, Charles Singer
English text: Anne White, Noel Kelly
Illustrations: Mariano Valsesia, Betti Ferrero

CHAPTER 1

Mary Expects a Baby

Emil Nolde (1867-1956)

White Amarylis with Mary and baby Jesus. Watercolor on Japanese paper.

About 4 B.C.*

Countryside around Nazareth in Israel.

At this time the Romans occupied Israel and many other Mediterranean countries. The capital city of Israel was Jerusalem. About 114 km (70 miles) to the north, among the hills of Galilee, was Nazareth, a small village with about 150 inhabitants. People from neighboring villages looked down on Nazarenes, as the inhabitants were called, saying, "Can anything good come from Nazareth?"

Mary, who was to be the mother of Jesus, lived in this village. Like most young Jewish women, she was already promised in marriage, to Joseph, a local carpenter. After the official celebration, Mary stayed with her parents for a year and then went to live with her husband. At this time Mary was expecting a baby.

* It seems strange to say *that Jesus was born B.C. (Before Christ). In fact, a monk from Rome, Denis, who established our calendar in the 6th century A.D., was mistaken by about four years in his calculations.*

A few years later

It was a few years later, after the crucifixion and resurrection of Jesus, that Luke wrote his Gospel account.

Luke began his Gospel by recounting an event that became known as the Annunciation, an event that clearly shows Jesus to be the Son of God.

Craftsman making a door in a small Israeli village.

The Annunciation

From the Gospel According to Luke (1:26-38)

And in the sixth month the angel Gabriel was sent from God unto a city of Galilee, named Nazareth, to a virgin espoused to a man whose name was Joseph, of the house of David; and the virgin's name was Mary. And the angel came in unto her, and said, Hail, thou that art highly favoured, the Lord is with thee: blessed art thou among women.

And when she saw him, she was troubled at his saying, and cast in her mind what manner of salutation this should be. And the angel said unto her, Fear not, Mary: for thou hast found favour with God. And, behold, thou shalt conceive in thy womb, and bring forth a son, and shalt call his name Jesus. He shall be great, and shall be called the Son of the Highest: and the Lord God shall give unto him the throne of his father David: And he shall reign over the house of Jacob for ever; and of his kingdom there shall be no end.

Then said Mary unto the angel, How shall this be, seeing I know not a man? And the angel answered and said unto her, The Holy Ghost shall come upon thee, and the power of the Highest shall overshadow thee: therefore also that holy thing which shall be born of thee shall be called the Son of God. And, behold, thy cousin Elizabeth, she hath also conceived a son in her old age: and this is the sixth month with her, who was called barren. For with God nothing shall be impossible. And Mary said, Behold the handmaid of the Lord; be it unto me according to thy word. And the angel departed from her.

Angels

The Scriptures teach us that holy angels are regarded as God's messengers (Hebrews 1:13-14).

David

He was Israel's greatest king, born in Bethlehem. He was king for 40 years, 1055-1015 B.C. The memory of David remained alive among the people of Israel and in difficult times they hoped for a new kingdom of David. During the Roman occupation, many people referred to Jesus as "Son of David."

Holy Spirit

The Holy Spirit is the third person in the Godhead. Also known as the "Spirit of God" or "the Spirit." The Holy Spirit was also present at creation (Genesis 1:2). When Jesus was conceived (Luke 1:35) the creative power of the Spirit (as in the Genesis creation) was given to the process of conception. The Holy Spirit is sometimes spoken of as "breath" or "wind" (Hebrew, *ruach*; Greek, *pnuema*).

5

Belonging to a Family

Birth

Jesus was born to die. He came to die on the cross for the sins of all those who would believe in Him. Through faith in Him we receive the new birth (John 3:3).

The same love

God loves us even more than our own parents can possibly love us. G has shown His great love toward us by sending Jesus into the world to di our place (John 3:16).

A surname

When we were born, we received a surname (last name) from our parents. With this name we become a member of the family of those born with the same name. God wants us to be part of His family. We become His children only when we believe and trust in His Son Jesus.

Baptism

Christians are baptized with the sign of water and the words "I baptize you in the name of the Father, of the Son and of the Holy Spirit" (Matthew 28:19).

By being baptized this way, Christians are showing God and the world that they want to be identified with the Father, the Son (Jesus), and the Holy Spirit. By being baptized, a Christian shows his or her willingness to obey God's commandments (Matthew 28:18-20).

One and Only

All, all, all:
the great and small,
humble and powerful,
sick and healthy,
rich and poor:

All, all, all:
whatever shade
of skin,
wherever they come from,
of all nations,
tribes and tongues . . .

God says to the world,
To the world,
"Believe on the Lord Jesus Christ, and
thou shalt be saved" (Acts 16:31).

"For God so loved the world, that he
gave his only begotten Son, that
whosoever believeth in him should not
perish, but have everlasting life. For
God sent not his Son into the world to
condemn the world; but that the
world through him might be saved.
He that believeth on him is not
condemned: but he that
believeth not is condemned
already, because he hath not
believed in the name of
the only begotten Son
of God"
(John 3:16-18).

7

A Child Is Born

Francisco de Zurbaran
(1598-1664)

The Adoration of the Shepherds,
1638

Born in a Stable

A caravan inn in the desert to the east of Jerusalem. It is a hostelry where caravans and travelers can find lodging.

Bethlehem was well known as the birthplace of King David. In his time the people of Israel were free, but a thousand years later, at the time of Mary and Joseph, the country was under Roman occupation. In order to keep control of the collection of taxes, the Emperor Caesar Augustus (27 B.C. - A.D. 14) ordered a nationwide census to be taken.

Joseph and Mary went to Bethlehem to register but were unable to find anywhere to stay. They eventually found a stable and it was there that Jesus was born, in an animal manger.

The Story of Jesus' Birth

At special occasions we take photos to help us remember the first look, the first smile, the first steps. In Jesus' day there were no pictures. At that time genealogies (or family lineages) were kept.

When Luke was writing about Jesus' birth he carefully documented this incredible event (Luke 1:1-4; 2:1-7). Under the inspiration of the Holy Spirit, Luke records for us the wonderful account of angels, a wondrous light, and songs of glory. Luke was not writing a detailed record of Jesus' birth. But he wants to show us the miraculous birth and life of Jesus, demonstrating the power of God in Christ.

Statue of the Emperor Augustus Caesar, on the Capital Hill in Rome, Italy.

* In what year was Jesus born?
The year 1998 signifies 1,998 years after the birth of Jesus. People have not always counted the years like that. Since the 6th century they decided to number the years left from the birth of Jesus. They made a mistake in the calculations of about six years. In reality, Jesus was born six years earlier. The year 1998 would be then the year 2004 (1998+6).

9

During the Night

From the Gospel According to Luke (2:1-14)

And it came to pass in those days, that there went out a decree from Caesar Augustus, that all the world should be taxed. (And this taxing was first made when Cyrenius was governor of Syria.) And all went to be taxed, every one into his own city.

And Joseph also went up from Galilee, out of the city of Nazareth, into Judaea, unto the city of David, which is called Bethlehem; (because he was of the house and lineage of David:) To be taxed with Mary his espoused wife, being great with child. And so it was, that, while they were there, the days were accomplished that she should be delivered. And she brought forth her firstborn son, and wrapped him in swaddling clothes, and laid him in a manger; because there was no room for them in the inn.

And there were in the same country shepherds abiding in the field, keeping watch over their flock by night. And, lo, the angel of the Lord came upon them, and the glory of the Lord shone round about them: and they were sore afraid. And the angel said unto them, Fear not: for, behold, I bring you good tidings of great joy, which shall be to all people. For unto you is born this day in the city of David a Saviour, which is Christ the Lord. And this shall be a sign unto you; Ye shall find the babe wrapped in swaddling clothes, lying in a manger.

And suddenly there was with the angel a multitude of the heavenly host praising God and saying, Glory to God in the highest, and on earth peace, good will toward men.

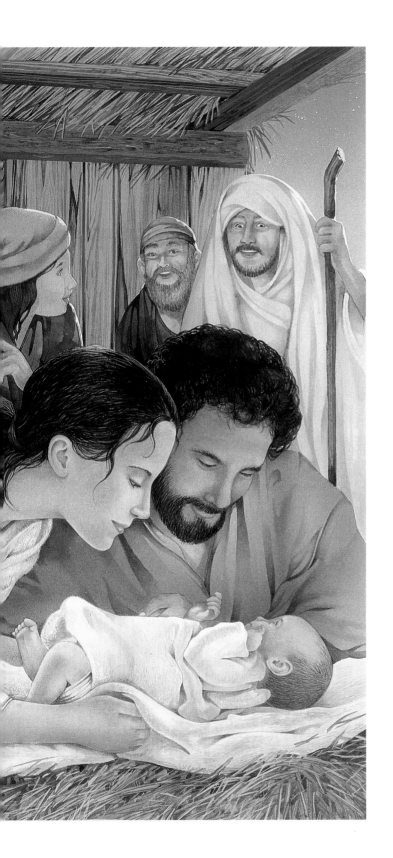

Noel

"Noel" (Christmas), the word comes from the original Latin meaning "day of birth." It now only means the day of the birth of Jesus.

Shepherds

To those who believe that God speaks first to the mighty, the kings, and the wealthy, Luke shows that God gives a special place to the despised, the poor, and the outcast, those not important in the eyes of society, like the shepherds of Bethlehem.

Christ

The people of the Bible expected a Saviour promised by God. This was to be the Messiah (from the Hebrew) or the Christ (from the Greek). Christians of all times and places recognized Jesus as the promised Messiah, or Christ.

God's Love for All

A Manger

Jesus was born in a manger not a palace,
not in gold or silk but in a poor place.

The Shepherds

In Jesus' day, shepherds were people who were often overlooked,
who were despised; yet, they were the first to see and worship
the Child of the Manger.

The Overlooked

The shepherds represent the "little ones," those "overlooked,"
the "poor" and the "deprived" at all times.

God's Mercy

Many people in the world lack food, love, freedom, homes, and care.
They have nothing, are helpless, and are waiting to be helped. God also
cares for and has mercy on them. His sun shines on the evil and the
good, and He sends rain on the just and the unjust (Matthew 5:45).

The Great Joy

God became a child, a human person on earth. This is the reason why
Christians rejoice at the telling or reading of the birth of Christ. God
came to share our life. God became one of us, yet without sin.

Son of God

How astounding!
How amazing
to be born in a stable
and cradled in a manger
when this is He
who comes to be
the Son of God, the
Almighty One.

People expect of God
riches and power:
the Christmas story
overturns that!

Jesus, the Son of God, is
born of a human mother to
become the brother of
every person who believes
and trusts in Him.

For when God became a
man in Christ, He came to
die for man's sins so that
man could be restored to a
right relationship with God.
As it is written, "For as in
Adam all die, even so in
Christ shall all be made
alive" (1 Corinthians
15:22).

The Magi from the East

Albrecht Dürer
(1471-1528)

Adoration of the Magi

© Alinari - Giraudon / Galerie des Offices, Florence, Italy

After the Birth of Jesus

This mosaic, showing the Magi offering gifts to the child Jesus, was made in the sixth century after Christ, and can be seen in the church of St. Apollinarius in Ravenna, Italy.

At the time of Jesus' birth, Herod the Great had been king of Judea for more than 30 years. He was a foreigner and became king with the support of the Roman Empire. Herod was hated, and he ruled through fear. His police were everywhere and he was afraid of losing his throne. Five days before his death he even had one of his own sons executed! Matthew's gospel account remembers the massacre of innocent children, ordered by Herod after he had heard about the birth of Jesus (Matthew 2:16-18).

The Gospel According to Matthew

Matthew's Gospel account was written not too long after the death and resurrection of the Lord Jesus. It was originally written for Christians of Jewish origins, or "Judeo-Christians." As they met together, people of other religions and other countries began to join them. Many of these were foreigners and strangers who were made welcome. In his gospel record, Matthew shows that when Jesus was born, strangers — the Magi* — were also led to Him.

The first Christians were often persecuted. By recalling the bloodthirsty, cruel figure of Herod, Matthew showed Christians that persecution was also a part of Jesus' life from the very beginning.

Sun setting over the Bethlehem area of Israel.

* The wise men who came to Jerusalem searching for the child who was "born king of the Jews" (Matthew 2:1-2) were of the "Magi," a class of royal scholars in Persia who were trained in astronomy and in all the wisdom of the ancient world. They were undoubtedly thoroughly familiar with the Old Testament Scriptures concerning the coming Redeemer and Saviour.

The Magi

From the Gospel According to Matthew (2:1-12)

Now when Jesus was born in Bethlehem of Judaea in the days of Herod the king, behold, there came wise men from the east to Jerusalem, saying, Where is he that is born King of the Jews? for we have seen his star in the east, and are come to worship him.

When Herod the king had heard these things, he was troubled, and all Jerusalem with him. And when he had gathered all the chief priests and scribes of the people together, he demanded of them where Christ should be born. And they said unto him, In Bethlehem of Judaea: for thus it is written by the prophet, And thou Bethlehem, in the land of Juda, art not the least among the princes of Juda: for out of thee shall come a Governor, that shall rule my people Israel.

Then Herod, when he had privily called the wise men, enquired of them diligently what time the star appeared. And he sent them to Bethlehem, and said, Go and search diligently for the young child; and when ye have found him, bring me word again, that I may come and worship him also. When they had heard the king, they departed; and, lo, the star, which they saw in the east, went before them, till it came and stood over where the young child was. When they saw the star, they rejoiced with exceeding great joy.

And when they were come into the house, they saw the young child with Mary his mother, and fell down, and worshipped him: and when they had opened their treasures, they presented unto him gifts; gold, and frankincense, and myrrh.

16

The Star

The star guided the Magi to Jesus, just as the angels showed the shepherds the way to Jesus in Luke's account. It would surely be appropriate for the most important event since the creation — namely the Incarnation of its Creator — to be signalled by this mighty spectacle of God's creative power. Whatever may have been the exact nature of this star at Christ's birth, it gave perfect witness to its Creator, Christ.

Gifts

The Magi were wealthy and Jesus came for the wealthy as well as the poor. These key representatives of the world's great Gentile (non-Jewish) nations came to fall down and worship the King of the Jews, knowing that one day every knee shall bow and every tongue confess that Jesus Christ, the Creator and Redeemer, is Lord (Philippians 2:10-11).

Searchers

The Magi
The Magi were "searchers," "explorers"
looking for the King of the Jews,
whose star they had seen.

Signs
The star in the sky was a
sign for the Magi to follow.

Strangers
The Magi were not from Bethlehem
or even the land of Israel.
They were strangers from a distant land.

The Whole World
The different nationality represented by
the Magi shows that the Child of the
Manger was born not just for His people,
but that He came for the whole world
(John 3:16).

18

Always Pilgrims

How can we know God?
How can we find God?
How can we believe in God?

Coming to God, and believing in
God is a pilgrim-like journey similar to
the one the Magi made to see Jesus.

Just as the Magi had to leave people,
places, and things, sometimes God calls
us to do the same in order to follow Him
obediently, just like the Magi did.

At the manger everyone is welcome:
shepherds and pagan strangers,
the poor and the rich,
people of different nations and status.

None can become God's children until
they have been born again by His Spirit.
All those who believe on the Lord Jesus
Christ, having repented of their sins,
are the children of God
(John 1:12-13; Romans 8:14-17;
1 John 3:1, 23).

The world can only flourish and
grow better if the gospel of
Jesus Christ is embraced
and people start taking
God at His word!

C H A P T E R • 4

The Early Years

Frederico Barocci (1535-1612)

The Circumcision

© Photo R.M.N., Musée du Louvre, Paris, France

Life in Nazareth

Shopping street in Nazareth, Israel.

Jesus spent most of His life in Nazareth and spoke Aramaic with a local accent. Among His first words would have been *immah* (mommy) and *abbah* (daddy). Jesus would have been taught the sacred language of the Jews, Hebrew, and He would have picked up some of the Greek and Latin used by soldiers, traders, and administrative officials.

Jesus shared village life. He would have watched His mother drawing water from the well, preparing yeast for baking bread, and seasoning food with salt. He would have seen Joseph, working as a craftsman, a carpenter. He would have watched shepherds at the head of their flocks, the sower scattering seed, and the vine grower pruning vines on the hillside. He played with His siblings and friends and grew up with them. Later they would find it difficult to remember Jesus as different. For some of them He remained "the carpenter's son."

Jesus was a Jew, and like every Jewish boy He was circumcised on the eighth day after His birth. His religious education started at home. On the Sabbath He would have gone to the synagogue with Joseph and heard about the Book of the Law (Hebrew, *Torah*), the first five books of our Bible today. All through the year, the Jewish feasts* would have helped Him to celebrate the story of the Jewish people.

Jewish man praying in Jerusalem, surrounded by the books of the Law.

Hebrew writing.

The Silence of the Gospels

The Gospels say very little about Jesus growing up in Nazareth. This is because they are not intended to be a biography of Jesus' private life. The Gospel writers are interested in His public life and the gospel message. What little they do say shows that Jesus' work in the world was built on this early life as He grew in wisdom and maturity.

* The New Year feast recalls the Creation, and the Passover feast the deliverance of the Israelites from Egypt. The Jewish feast of Pentecost is a reminder of the gift of the law given to Moses on Mount Sinai. The Feast of the Tabernacles or Booths commemorates the journey through the desert from Egypt to the Promised Land.

Growing Up

From the Gospel According to Luke (2:21-24, 39-40)

And when eight days were accomplished for the circumcising of the child, his name was called Jesus, which was so named of the angel before he was conceived in the womb.

And when the days of her purification according to the law of Moses were accomplished, they brought him to Jerusalem, to present him to the Lord; (As it is written in the law of the Lord, Every male that openeth the womb shall be called holy to the Lord;) And to offer a sacrifice according to that which is said in the law of the Lord, A pair of turtledoves, or two young pigeons.

And when they had performed all things according to the law of the Lord, they returned into Galilee, to their own city Nazareth. And the child grew, and waxed strong in spirit, filled with wisdom: and the grace of God was upon him.

Jesus

His name means "God saves." "Joshua" is Hebrew for Jesus, and it was a common name among Jews in honor of Joshua who led the Israelites into the Promised Land. People did not have surnames, and so Jesus would have been known as "Jesus, son of Joseph."

Circumcision

Circumcision is the removal of the male's foreskin. It is an ancient religious rite for Jews and is a sign of the covenant between God and Israel (Genesis 17:12; Luke 2:21).

Two Doves

Leviticus 12:8 required the sacrifice of lamb to be offered. Mary was too poor to offer the usual lamb as a sacrifice. The Law required that someone who was poor at least offer two doves, which she did.

The Steps of Life

A Baby

Jesus was a baby like any other baby (only without Adam's sin-nature): crying, laughing, sleeping, dreaming. . . . He needed to be taken care of, to be fed, comforted, changed, cradled, hugged. . . .

The Customs of His People

Jesus was born among the Jewish people. He was educated according to the customs of His people and learned their way of life.

Learning

Every child needs to be helped and guided through the first steps of life, to learn the words of a language, to distinguish colors and objects.

Discovering

For a little child, every day, every place is a novelty. People, objects, sounds, light, and dark . . . a child's eyes widen, it is excited by each new discovery. . . .

The Experience of Life

Tasting water, touching soil, smiling, hugging, discovering His limits, learning obedience . . . Jesus had to experience for himself.

The God-man: His Humanity

Parents, family, friends, and many others are needed to help a child take those first steps in life.

Jesus was a little child. He grew like other children, yet He was sinless.

Jesus knew the same joys, the same difficulties, the same struggles we know (Hebrews 4:15; 7:26), yet He was perfect.

By God becoming a man in Christ, He can be sensitive to our temptations and struggles. His humanity, as well as His deity, makes Him a fully capable high priest (Hebrews 4:15).

This is precisely why the Son of God has come among us: to reveal God to mankind, and to become one of us in order to make the atonement for our sins. Because He was both God and man He could then die in our place for our sins.

Adolescence

Van Bosch Aken Hieronimus
(about 1450-1516)

Jesus among the Teachers

© Photo R.M.N. - Jean, Musée du Louvre, Paris, France

Jesus at 12 Years Old

Scale model of the city of Jerusalem.

Going to Jerusalem was an extraordinary adventure for a 12 year old from a little village in the northern part of the land of Israel. Jerusalem was the capital, the Holy City. Jesus went with Mary and Joseph for the Feast of the Passover. He would have walked across the countryside with the crowds of people going to Jerusalem, making friends, entering the city filled with pilgrims, and finally seeing the temple* and there He would have joined in the week of festivities.

Teachers (called "rabbis") taught and answered questions under the colonnades of The Temple. Many pilgrims, young and old, would stop to listen to the teachers. Jesus, even though He was only 12, joined one of the groups and spoke with the teachers.

Luke's Gospel Account

Jesus lived in Nazareth for about 30 years and Luke tells us about the only event mentioned from those years, the journey to Jerusalem.

Luke wants his readers to know from the beginning that Jesus is the Son of God, and that He is both the promised Messiah to Israel and the Redeemer of the world.

Luke wants his readers to understand who Jesus really was and who His real Father is, that is, God. In this Gospel record Luke shows us that some people found that difficult to believe or understand. Even Mary and Joseph did not fully understand what Jesus meant when He said, "I must be about my Father's business" (Luke 1:49).

One of the gates of the Jerusalem wall, Israel.

* The Temple
The temple was the most important religious place for Jews. A large square was surrounded with colonnades and a central building divided into three main areas: the outer courtyard, the Holy Place (sanctuary), and the Holy of Holies (symbolizing the presence of God).

Jesus among the Teachers

From the Gospel According to Luke (2:41-45)

Now his parents went to Jerusalem every year at the feast of the passover. And when he was twelve years old, they went up to Jerusalem after the custom of the feast. And when they had fulfilled the days, as they returned, the child Jesus tarried behind in Jerusalem; and Joseph and his mother knew not of it. But they, supposing him to have been in the company, went a day's journey; and they sought him among their kinsfolk and acquaintance. And when they found him not, they turned back again to Jerusalem, seeking him. And it came to pass, that after three days they found him in the temple, sitting in the midst of the doctors, both hearing them, and asking them questions. And all that heard him were astonished at this understanding and answers. And when they saw him, they were amazed and his mother said unto him, Son, why has thou dealt with us? Behold, thy father and I have sought thee sorrowing.

And he said unto them, How is it that ye sought me? Wist ye not that I must be about my Father's business? And they understood not the saying which he spake unto them.

And he went down with them, and came to Nazareth, and was subject unto them: but his mother kept all these sayings in her heart and Jesus increased in wisdom and stature (or age), and in favour with God and man.

Passover

This feast celebrated God's miraculous deliverance of the Israelites from slavery in Egypt.

Father

Jesus was blessed with a caring earthly father, Joseph, but prepared to fulfill the will of God, His heavenly Father.

Doctors

Jesus was able to debate with the learned "doctors" (rabbis) about Scripture, even at this young age.

Consider This . . .

Childhood

A child is taken by the hand. Children learn to make decisions. Their parents do this for them first. A child is guided. . . .

Adolescence

The adolescent wants to choose his/her own way of life. During this time the understanding of choices and consequences is developed. The time will come when everyone must make their own choices and decisions.

Talking

Jesus participates in the adults' discussions. To the scholars of the law, Jesus, a boy of 12, also has something to say about God and the way to love Him. . . .

Respect

Even though Jesus is the Son of God, He showed respect and submission to Mary and Joseph.

Obeying God's Will

Jesus decides to stay at the temple. He was there in keeping with God's will. Jesus was there in obedience to God, His real Father, to fulfill His mission on earth as the Son of God.

Growing

Growing is not just about getting stronger and bigger. . . .

Growing is about becoming capable of talking, thinking, living and making decisions according to God's Word — the Holy Bible.

Growing is about becoming capable of listening carefully, accepting advice, weighing the pros and cons, having the courage to accept the consequences of difficult choices as we check them against God's Word.

Growing is about learning to love and give the best of ourselves, and not, like a child, getting everything just for our own pleasure, but for God's glory. . . .

Growing is difficult. It is a long process, a never-ending task.

It doesn't always have a lot to do with age. . . . Growing is about learning to trust God in order to become the person He wants us to be.

Growing means searching for God wholeheartedly, obeying Him wholeheartedly, and continuing to trust God wholeheartedly.

The Origin of Christmas

There is no indication in the New Testament that the early Christians observed Christmas at all. It is not surprising, therefore, that there have been various groups of Christians, both in the past and the present, who have reacted against Christmas and New Year celebrations so vigorously as to reject them altogether and to prohibit their members from taking any part in them. Certainly the Saturnalian aspects of these celebrations ought to be avoided by Christians, as these are clearly pagan in both origin and character.

The English word *Christmas* can be traced back to the Old English words *Christes maesse*, meaning "the mass or festival of Christ." Although many churches throughout the world do not adhere to the Catholic "mass" or "feast," they take the opportunity during this time and season to recount the birth of the Saviour.

The Date of Christ's Birth

Nobody knows the exact day on which Jesus was born. The Scriptures do not give us the day or the time of year that He was born. December in Israel is the height of the rainy season when neither flocks nor shepherds would have been out at night in the cold fields of Bethlehem.

Perhaps the most probable date, though no one really knows, is about September 29. This would have been a good time for the Roman census, with the weather warm and most of the harvest in, and with people traveling anyway. Shepherds would still have their flocks in the field, whereas none of this seems at all likely in the wintertime.

The Nativity Scene

In 1223, Francis of Assisi made the first nativity scene. It was in a cave in the little village of Greccio in Italy. He wanted to show the poverty into which Jesus was born.

Noel: Dies Natalis

Some people sing carols about Christmas and use the word "noel." This comes from two Latin words, *dies natalis*, which mean "birthday." Noel is also connected with a French word which means "new" (*nouvelle*), showing that the celebration of Christmas really is the Good News of the Saviour people had been long waiting for.

Advent

During the four weeks before December 25 some churches get ready for Christmas by reading the Bible, praying and singing, giving alms to the poor, and decorating their houses. Lots of families make an advent wreath by weaving small branches of evergreens together. They put four candles on it, to be lit as each Sunday of Advent comes along, to show that the light is getting brighter as Christmas approaches.

Ways of Celebrating Christmas

These days, Christmas is celebrated all over the world. Every country has its own special customs. But these different customs really end up borrowing from each other and becoming jumbled together. From Lapland to Australia, from France to Russia, from Italy to Canada, many people erect the Christmas tree, leave presents by the chimney, have cakes and sweets specially made for the feast, place candles on the window sills, and have their streets lit up.

The Saddest Day in the History of the Universe

Do you know what was the saddest day of all time? It was an event that affected everything in the universe. In fact, this incident affected the stars, the dirt, the animals, the plants, and you and me! Nothing in this creation was untouched.

In Genesis 3 we are given the historical account of how the first man, Adam, disobeyed his Creator. The devil (a rebellious angel), in the form of a serpent, was able to get Adam to disobey God. Adam ate the fruit from the tree of the knowledge of good and evil — the only tree God had told him he was not to eat from.

Adam's disobedience is called sin — and as a result of this act, everything changed. From this time on the ground was cursed, thorns and thistles started to grow — but the saddest thing of all was that now death entered creation.

Before sin, Adam and his wife, Eve, had a perfect relationship with their Creator God. But because God is holy, Adam's sin destroyed this perfect harmony. God had warned Adam that to disobey Him in eating from this one tree would result in death.

Now Adam and Eve were cut off from God — and their bodies also started to die. The animals also started to die — in fact, everything in the universe started to fall apart. God had judged sin! And because Adam was the head of the human race, then all of his descendants would inherit his sin nature, and thus all humans were condemned to die. Even though the human body would die, because man is made in God's image with an immortal soul — all would live forever, but separated from God. What a terrible, horrible situation.

The Happiest Day in the Universe

However, God did something very, very special so we could have the opportunity of living in a perfect relationship with our Creator once again.

Because a man brought sin, and thus death, into the world — a man was needed to pay the penalty for sin, and thus provide a way for mankind to come back to God. But this man would have to be a perfect man — and yet now all people would be sinners! What was the solution?

God provided a wonderful solution. He sent His Son to become a man — a perfect man. Around 2,000 years ago in a little town called Bethlehem, the Lord Jesus Christ was born.

The reason He came to earth to be one of us (but without sin) was to "destroy the works of the devil" (1 John 3:8). And He did this when He died on a cross and was raised from the dead — thus paying the penalty for sin, and destroying the works of the devil. Now all those who come to the Lord Jesus in faith and repentance, believing in the work He did on the cross, will spend eternity in heaven with their Creator!

The account of the birth of the Lord Jesus Christ when He became flesh is often only read at Christmas time. But this blessed event needs to be recounted over and over again lest we forget the wonder of it all — that our Creator should step into human history to save sinners like you and me who deserve nothing but judgment for our rebellion against God.

As you read this book time and time again, never cease to marvel at the happiest day in the universe!

Ken Ham
Executive Director
Answers in Genesis

Answers in Genesis is a non-profit, Christ-centered, evangelistic ministry.

An Awesome Adventure Titles Now Available:

- Jesus the Child
- Jesus is Calling

Upcoming Titles Available Soon:

- The Creation Story
- Abraham's Family
- Jesus Heals
- Who is Jesus
- Moses
- The Promised Land

TEXT

Albert HARI - Charles SINGER

PHOTOGRAPHY

Frantisek ZVARDON

Alsace MÉDIA

Patrice THÉBAULT

Jesus
the Child

EDITED BY
KEN HAM

ILLUSTRATIONS

Mariano VALSESIA

Betti FERRERO

MIA. Milan Illustrations Agency

FIRST PRINTING, FEBRUARY 1998

Copyright © 1998 by Master Books
for the CBA US edition.

For information write: Master Books, P.O. Box 727, Green Forest, AR 72638

ISBN: 0-89051-197-7

Master Books

ÉDITIONS
DU SIGNE
© ÉDITIONS DU SIGNE 1997